ATTENTION THERAPY

John D. Michael

Therapy with children from

12 months of age to 4 years of age.

Overview of Attention Therapy:

In order to develop good speech and conversation skills, a child needs to pay attention to the speaker and respond back when spoken to. Attention Therapy is a method that can be used to teach young children how to pay attention to you when you talk to them. It is a method that can teach young children how to respond back to you, to talk to you, and how to follow your directions. It consists of a series of activities that encourage children to look at you, and to listen to you when you talk, instead of ignoring you. It encourages children to respond more regularly to their name, to respond back to you, to talk to you, and to follow basic instructions. The Attention Therapy activities start at a very basic level, and then over time gradually become more complicated after the child has learned the basic foundation skills.

The focus and the goal of Attention Therapy are to teach children that parents and caretakers are more important than screens and toys. The goal is also to teach children that looking at and listening to an adult is more important that looking at or listening to a screen or a toy. This method does not just encourage children to follow your routines or your directions the way some other behavior health therapies do; instead it teaches children how to look at you, how to listen to you, how to pay attention to you, how to look at you to get help instead of just pulling you, how to respond back to you, and how to talk to you.

This method has been used for many years in the Early Intervention program. It has been generally used with children between the ages of 12 months and 4 years, who show delays in responding to their name, who show delays in attending to other people, who show delays in joint attention skills, and who show delays in receptive language and expressive language skills. These children are more interested in doing what they want to do when they want to do it instead of doing what the parents or caretaker wants them to do, or doing what typically developing children usually can do at their age. These children are often described as "very independent," as often "ignoring" their parents, and as having a speech delay.

This method can be used over several months, or even much longer. The length of time depends upon how fast the child responds and how fast the child learns the skills. It is somewhat like learning a new language or a new skill. The more exposure to the method and the more practice, every day, the faster the skills are learned. The faster the child learns, the shorter will be the need for therapy, and the faster attention, responses, and verbal conversation occurs.

OK?

Now ... Pay Attention!

Pay Attention to Attention Therapy!

Table of Contents

Table of Contents

Part One: Introduction to Attention Therapy

This is a method that can teach young children how to pay attention, how to respond back to you, and how to develop better talking skills, communication skills, and social skills.

Babies look directly at another person's face, even before they are able to make meaningful sounds. They focus on a face. This may be called socialization, recognition, or attention, but it is the first, the most basic, and the most important skill needed for the development of good speech and language development. It is considered a necessary basic stage for typical development. Next, typically developing babies interact with you. They recognize that you are very important. They make facial movements and body motions that draw you into their world. Next, typically developing babies respond back to you. They smile back to you, they frown, they laugh, they cry, and they move their face and body, in response to your attention.

These three basic skills, looking at your face, recognition of your importance, and responding back to you, must continue to develop more fully over a child's first and second years of life, as they become the basic foundation upon which a child's speech, language, and conversation skills develop. The non-verbal facial gestures, body movements, plus attention to another person must develop first, before good vocal speech and language can develop. When something interferes with one of these basic skills, speech, language and conversation development are hampered. Social development and learning skills are often are hampered as well.

Pre-lingual communication usually develops in infancy. It consists of vocalizations, gestures, eye movements/gazes, or other non-verbal movements to get attention and to communicate before the development of spoken language. It may also continue in children who have a hearing impairment, who exhibit a speech delay, who do not speak or who cannot speak.

Some examples of pre-lingual communication include: Vocal babbling; pointing to the item you want; gesturing for someone to follow you; putting your hand up to gesture, "stop;" pointing your thumb up to gesture "OK;" tapping someone on the arm or shoulder, or clapping your hands to get attention; moving your head sideways for "No!" or nodding your head for "Yes;" smiling at someone; moving your lips to make a sad face; lifting your eyelids or moving your eyes to agree with someone; winking your eye to disagree; sticking your tongue out to disagree, and moving your body to get someone to hurry up. Of course, there are cultural considerations and differences. As you see, pre-lingual communication can be non-verbal expressions, can be gestures, and can be vocal sounds that are not speech. Sounds may be made, but the major message of communication is non-verbal, without verbal sounds, and without speaking words.

Pre-lingual skills can occur with or without the development of the three most basic skills mentioned above. When pre-lingual skills develop **after** a child focuses on a face, desires interaction with another person, and wants to respond to that other person, good speech and language skills often develop. But, when the pre-lingual skills develop without the development of a child focusing on the face of another person, without a child desiring more than physical interaction with another person, and without the need to respond to another person, appropriate speech and language development does not usually occur. Social skills and learning skills may be delayed as well.

Some parents tell me that their two year old child is "very independent." "He gets things for himself." That does not require communication. An example is when a child thinks, "I can get it by myself, "or "I do not need anyone to help me." Then there is no need for communication. The child just gets the item himself. Another example is when a child pulls you over, and you imagine what he wants, and you hand it to him. Here again there is little need for communication. You may ask, "What do you want?" But, if you ask, the child doesn't know how to respond, except to cry or tantrum more. If getting it himself does not work, he gets upset, because he doesn't know how to communicate to another person for help, or how to look in your direction to get your attention. This child has not

7

yet developed the basic foundation skills of looking at a face, recognizing your importance, and wanting to respond back to you.

Therefore, to develop appropriate speech and language skills, a child must first develop the basic foundation skills to 1) focuses on a face, 2) desire interaction with an important person, and 3) want to respond back to another person. Next, and equally important, 4) a child must understand (or be taught) joint attention. Joint attention skills are extremely difficult to understand if the child has not mastered the earlier first three basic skills. Not understanding, or not learning, any of these four basic skills interferes with how to use speech and language in an appropriate manner.

Joint attention is a special kind of attention. It is when two people recognize that they share a focus on something interesting and relate to each other about that interest. One example is when a child looks at another person in order to share a thought with that other person; not just focusing attention to a toy, to an object or to an action. Joint attention is the process of attending to another person, and interacting with that person in a back and forth manner. Ideas and thoughts are shared and there is back and forth communication; a brief "non-verbal conversation." That back and forth communication, the brief conversation, is non-verbal at first. Speech develops later. Without joint attention development, speech development is often delayed, or it develops inappropriately. Both non-verbal communication (pre-lingual skills), and joint attention skills develop together during the first year of life. They are often intertwined, and together they are called "non-verbal joint attention.

How can you tell if your child understands non-verbal joint attention? When you hold a wanted toy or food in your hand and your child looks at your face for several seconds and waits for you to give the toy, that is the beginning of joint attention. If your child reaches for the toy and does not look at you, the first step in joint attention has not yet been developed. If you hold the wanted toy up next to your face again, and your child still reaches for the toy and does not look at you longer than for one second, the four basic skills above are not understood, and need to be taught.

Once non-verbal joint attention skills are developed and are used every day, speech skills build upon this foundation, and expand. Once your child realizes the importance of looking toward another person for help, and the importance of connecting non-verbally with another person, your child will then realize the need to communicate with, and then to talk to that other person. Then, the desire to talk will come from your child himself, or from herself.

Most parents focus on their child's speech. They focus on speech therapy or sign language in order to encourage their child to communicate. They do not realize that the therapy will be so much more effective when their child focuses on their face, pays attention to them, is able to follow directions, and is able to respond to the therapist.

Experience has shown that if speech develops without a child first learning good non-verbal joint attention skills, the speech is often mechanical, mostly labeling what the child sees (blue, apple, triangle, yellow ball, dinosaur, one- two- three), statements of facts or statements of needs (milk, aqua, juice, up, out) or thoughts expressed without connection with or without consideration of others (Go home now!, You have big feet.). The child often talks when he wants to talk, not when someone else wants the child to talk.

However, when speech does develop after the development of non-verbal joint attention, (I.e.: the non-verbal connection with others and sharing thoughts with others) speech and language develops more appropriately, and back and forth conversation also develops more appropriately.

Note also that non-verbal movements and non-verbal facial expressions often alter the meaning of a spoken statement. A blink of an eye lid, or a frown, or a smile, or a head nod, often changes the meaning to the opposite of what has just been said. Non-verbal joint attention is a basic skill; part of the basic foundation. It often adds to, changes, or over rides, other forms of communication.

Non-verbal joint attention, itself, is built upon three steps: The first step is attention to another person. The next step is to look at what I want. You see me look at you, and then see me look at the object I find interesting. The third step is looking back to you as if to say will you join me, or as if to say, "Isn't that interesting?" I am sharing my interests with you and hope you will agree with me. This is much more than having you help me get what I want. This is sharing ideas and interests with you. Sometimes the three steps are in a different manner. First, I look at what interests me, then I look at you to show you my interest, and then, look back at the object so we look at it together. Then, I look back at you again, to get your smile or your agreement about my interest.

One example of a conversation using non-verbal joint attention is when you are standing in a line and someone "cuts" in front of you. Instead of yelling at that person, you turn towards her, wave your hand or stamp your foot and look at her face to get her attention. When she looks back at you, you point to the back of the line. She responds back by pointing to the people next to her as if to say," I am with them." You don't believe her, and you nod your head and point to the end of the line again. She looks at your face again, and she nods her head for "No!", and stays put. You both just had a multi-step, back and forth non-verbal joint attention conversation. And you understood each other without talking.

Non-verbal joint attention does not depend upon what language, or languages, a person hears during the day. What it does depend upon is the sustained attention given to the non-verbal and verbal languages heard. Any language spoken by a nearby person is included, but definitely not music, songs or languages spoken by a screen, a game, or a toy. Children in many countries learn several languages by being exposed to them while growing up. Some young children may show a slight delay in acquiring speech in the multiple languages when they are under 4 years of age. With the development of good non-verbal joint attention skills, that mild delay soon disappears.

Most children develop non-verbal joint attention skills under one year of age, and have very good use of it by 12-15 months of age. Children who have not developed these skills by 15-18 months of age, have difficulty attending to instructions for their age level, and have difficulty developing typical speech and conversation kills.

Due to the joint attention delay, speech therapy alone often shows slower progress, because the child is not attending to the task, and is not following the directions of the teacher. This is very similar to you being offered lessons about learning a new skill or a new language, but you do not care, you are not interested, and you do not pay attention to the teacher. However, after you do pay attention to the teacher, once you find it fun, you learn faster. So does a child.

Typically developing young children often communicate between each other with non-verbal joint attention. They follow the other children, and laugh, and have fun. They run about, chase each other, and change activities by watching the non-verbal movements of the other children. Some children, however, appear social, and appear to follow what the other children are doing, but they do not attend to adults, they do not look at faces, and they really do not exhibit non-verbal joint attention. These young children prefer running about after other children, or doing their own thing, rather than attending to an adult or following directions given by an adult. These children are helped by learning better non-verbal joint attention skills.

To use sign language a person is required to use non-verbal gestures to communicate. The non-verbal gestures, signs, should not be directed to the wall, but to the other person's face. Often the non-verbal signs are also accompanied by facial expressions or vocal sounds. A child who does not pay enough attention to a face has difficulty learning these skills, and may just mimic your hand motions. The negative aspect of using non-verbal hand signs is that the message is not often focusing on people's faces, but on their hands. We don't talk to our hands, or to other people's hands; we talk to people's faces. Sign language is not a substitute for learning non-verbal joint attention.

Therefore, when someone uses hand signs to communicate, it is important that they must look at the other person's face while they sign or gesture, and the other person must look back at their face, too. That also applies to any social physical movement or gesture such as a "high-five," a wave, an "elbow touch," a pull, or a physical tap. The movement must be, should be, accompanied with a look to the other person's face.

The foundation upon which basic communication is built is: 1) focusing on a face, 2) desire to get the attention of an important person, 3) wanting to respond back to that other person, 4) using non-verbal joint attention communication skills, and 5) adding speech to the non-verbal joint attention skills in order to build a back and forth conversation.

Hey There, Pay Attention!

Pay Attention to Attention Therapy!

Frequently Asked Questions

How old should a child be to begin using Attention Therapy?

> Attention Therapy is best started with children between the ages of 12 months and 3 years of age. It probably can be used with children 4 years of age and older, but we have not had that experience.

How often should I do each activity with my child?

> It is similar to learning a new language, or a new skill. The more often it is practiced, the more it is learned. Plus, if it is fun and enjoyable, it is learned even faster. Do an activity many times a day; at least 4-5 times in a group, at least 10 groups, even more, spread out over a day, every day. Make it part of your routine. Remember to incorporate several "looks" and back and forth "facial responses" into every activity, and into all play. Include it into every play with cars, with balls, dolls, boxes, songs, dance steps, having fun, "roughhousing,," dressing, diaper changing, bathing, eating, parallel play, shopping, walking about indoors and outdoors; incorporate it smoothly into everything you do!

How can I know if a certain activity or a procedure is helping?

> Observe your child. Watch your child's interests and activities over several weeks. Does he look at your face more, now? Does he interact with you and respond back to you more now, than before? Does he listen to you more, or follow more directions, now? Do you notice improvement in other areas, too? If some improvement is noticed, then the procedure may be working.

How long will it take before my child improves?

Some children catch on to the activities within a few weeks, some take a few months to respond. It all depends upon your child and which activities your child likes to do. Try several activities as described below. Spend time on the ones that seem to work. Remember that many children refuse to cooperate at first. They get upset when things change, and don't go their way. You may need to do activities over several months for better results. It really depends upon on how fast your child learns the skills. With repetitive, consistent daily activities, most children catch on, and then, over time, show much improvement.

Which activities or what methods are the best for my child?

Some children respond better to some specific therapies, and some children respond better to other therapies. It depends upon your child's interests, and your child's personality. It will change with time. Take time, and watch your child. Observe what interests your child, and then use some of the methods below that seem to work best. Find out what activities your child is able to do a little bit, and then begin asking your child to do that activity first. Then try another. It may take a few weeks, before you will see any change.

What about day care/preschool?
What about care during the day by a sitter or a nanny?
What about care by another family member?

Care during the day by another person is necessary for many families. Is the daycare person willing to help out with the therapy, or is your child allowed to watch TV or a screen for several hours? Is your child allowed to do whatever he wants to do? Spending several hours during the day doing whatever he wants to do, without therapy, makes it more difficult for the therapy to be given in the evening at home, when everyone is tired and under more stress.

Besides, in the evening at home, both you and your child wants to be relaxed together, not under more stress. Learning to pay attention is similar to learning a new language or a new skill, the more often you practice, the faster you learn. Plus, if it is fun and enjoyable, you learn even faster.

Your child may learn to follow the routines and join the other children at play. You may be told that your child is following the rules, but he is probably not learning to communicate face to face. Once your child pays better attention to your face, responds back to you, and follows your directions, then he will learn more from other adults and children, and also learn to communicate better with you and with others.

Please encourage all your family members, and the caretakers at day care/preschool to help out with the therapy, as much as possible.

What about being with other children so he can see what they do, and copy their behavior?

If your child attends to you, watches you, and follows your directions, then he will watch and listen to other adults and children, and learn from them. If your child does not pay attention to you, and does not yet follow several of your directions, then he will just copy the activities and the movement of other children that interest him. Your child will not learn to communicate face to face. Once your child learns to pay better attention to your face, realizes your importance, responds back to you, and follows your directions, then he will learn more from other adults and from the activities of other children. He will also learn to communicate better with you and with others.

Part Two: Attention Therapy

Here is a method that teaches children to pay attention, to focus on a face, to desire to have the attention of another person, to respond to the other person, to develop non-verbal joint attention, and to develop better talking, skills, communication skills, and social skills.

The focus and goal of Attention Therapy is to teach children that parents and caretakers are more important than screens and toys. The goal is also to teach children that looking at and listening to an adult is more important that looking at or listening to a screen or a toy. This method does not just encourage children to follow your routines or your directions the way many other behavior health therapies do; instead it teaches children how to look at you, how to listen to you, how to pay attention to you, how to look at you to get help, how to respond back to you, and how to talk to you.

In the previous section we discussed the foundation upon which basic communication is built: 1) focusing on a face, 2) desire to get the attention of another important person, 3) wanting to respond to that other person, and 4) understanding and using non-verbal joint attention communication skills. It is recommended that the important points discussed in that article be reviewed so that the following ideas and methods are better understood.

The basic steps that children must learn are divided into five levels; each level has a goal built upon the basic foundation. A child does not have to do each and every step in one level in succession, but your child should not skip levels. The goal is to learn the general idea of each level, and to be able to use the skills described on a daily basis, before going on to the next level. **Find out what activities your child is able to do on a regular basis, and then begin asking your child to do activities on that level. That way your child starts with success and confidence, not with challenges and failure.**

For those of you who skipped the introduction [and for those of you who did read it]:

These four pictures are what the goal of Attention Therapy may look like, but of different age, different color, or different style. The goal is to teach your child to look at you, to listen to you, to respond back to you, to gesture back to you, to talk to you, and hopefully to have a back and forth communication with you.

Teran Studios/Shutterstock.com

These four pictures are what the goal of Attention Therapy may look like, but of different age, different color, or different style. The goal is to teach your child to look at you, to listen to you, to respond back to you, to gesture back to you, to talk to you, and hopefully to have a back and forth communication with you.

Monkey Business/Shutterstock.com

Level 1: The Goal is for Your Child to Focus on Your Face, Not on a Toy.

1. In this first level, we are not encouraging your child to speak, or to talk. We are not encouraging your child to make sounds. Instead of recognizing the need to teach non-verbal joint attention skills first, before speech, many parents focus on directly teaching speech, without understanding the need for first developing the child's attention skills. Most communication is non-verbal and all communication requires attention. The focus of this level is to teach how important it is to focus on a face, and to pay attention.

2. The importance of sustained attention, listening to, and focusing on another person by the young child is often overlooked. Some children look only briefly at the person talking to them. Some children do not look at all, even when their name is called several times. Notice how you look toward another person and that person looks toward you, when you talk to each other. Looking into someone's eyes, "eye contact," is not important; many people find that very uncomfortable. Looking toward someone's face when you talk is important, as that is where you direct your speech, toward someone's face; not to the wall, or to toy, or to a screen. Looking toward the person who is talking, and listening to that person is also so important that it is necessary to achieve that skill, before adequate speech, language, conversation, social, and even learning skills can fully develop.

3. Be sure your child has good hearing ability, and good vision. Does your child respond to voices, music, and sounds appropriately? Does your child move to the TV, phone or screen when it "speaks" or makes sounds? A hearing test and a vision test often give the final answer.

4. Does your child have adequate oral-motor skills? If your child has any oral-motor disorder, difficulty such as drinking from a cup with or without a spout, sucking liquids through a straw and swallowing it, chewing and swallowing foods and blowing air from the mouth, it is important to consult with the therapist about which activities are appropriate.

22

5. Notice how long your child looks in your direction, and at your face, when you talk to him. And notice how long your child looks toward you, when he is trying to get help from you. If your child pulls you, but does not look towards your face, or looks away within a second or two, more development in this first level is needed. It is very important to get your child's attention before responding to his wants. Encourage your child to look in your direction in some way as below, before you respond to his wants or before you give an instruction or a direction.

6. Getting attention: Get in front of your child! You may gently tap your child's nose, then your nose. Or put your child's finger or hand on your nose briefly. Clap your hands, make a noise, gently touch your child's shoulder or arm, or do what you already know to get his attention, such as turning on or turning off a screen, TV or music, flashing room lights, or even opening the door to the refrigerator. Get in your child's way so he has to recognize you are there. Even if your child pushes you out of the way, he is recognizing that you are there. Repeat getting into his way, calling his name, and gently lift his head up so that he briefly looks toward your face. When your child looks in your direction, immediately move out of the way, and get/give the thing he wants. Repeat and repeat. Gradually, your child will understand to look at you (even briefly) in order to get what he wants. The goal is to connect with your face.

7. Timing is important! It is extremely difficult to get a good response when you, your child, or anyone, is tired, stressed, or upset, especially in the evening time. It is even more difficult to get a good response in the evening if your child does not practice during the day, and instead is allowed to do what he wants. The more often you practice some skill, the better you learn it. Therefore, we strongly encourage day caretakers, and parents to incorporate the 'looking at a face' skills, and the 'non-verbal joint attention' skills into your child's everyday routines, every day activities, dressing, bathing, diaper changing, eating, playing, building, singing, preparing to go outside, at the park, etc. etc., as explained below.

8. Be a model for your child. Frequently get on your child's level when you talk to him. Bend over, or sit on the floor. Talk slowly. Smile. Nod your head. Always talk directly to your child's face, not the back of his head. We all learn to talk by looking at a person's face; talking to another face. We do not learn to talk by talking to a toy, to a screen, or to the back of someone's head. If you need to move around to get in front of your child, do so. If you need to move your child around, do so; turn the stroller, the chair, or the toys so your child is facing you. Your child should see your face when you talk. Your child needs to learn that it is important to direct his attention to a face; your face. Instead of yelling, "No!" to the back of your child's head, quickly move around (or move your child around) and talk to his face. Get in front of your child, and say to his face, "We are not opening the door now." And don't let the door open. When dressing or bathing or giving instructions, talk to a face, "We are getting dressed." Or, "We are going to the park." Show many facial expressions to your child. The goal is sustained "looks" of attention to your face, recognition of your face, and acceptance of another person, instead of focusing on a hand, a toy, or an action. Do not insist any child look at your face, or even your eyes, when you are angry or you are lecturing to your child. No one likes that, and it makes looking to you when you want attention more difficult.

9. Focus attention to you. Children focus on what interests them. Make yourself interesting. Make yourself important. Turn off the screen, the TV, the video, and anything that may distract your child's attention away from you. Ideally, remove the many toys and games that are sitting there for your child to attend to any time he wants, instead of to you. Find out what makes our child laugh. Do it. Get him to look at you, and to laugh at you, at your face. Be silly, act funny, play peek-a-boo, make a noise; do whatever it takes (without harshness) to get your child's attention.

You may on occasion say, "Look," but at this level do not expect understanding of your words; demonstrate, act, and attract instead. Motivate your child by using favorite books, snack foods, fruits, drinks, toys, puzzles, games, music, dance, songs, etc. even, candy, ice cream, or treats, and yes, short videos (as below). Use these strong motivators to reward your child for attending to you a little bit longer, and on expanding those basic attention skills as descried below. These strong motivators may be used to get attention between meals, at meal times, and during routine daily activities when attention is wanted as described below. Notice what happens. When your child holds attention to you a bit longer on a regular basis, his activity and his body movements become more focused, and less scattered.

10. Using strong motivator snack foods such as crackers, fruits, treats, candy, ice cream, etc.: Children, who are given a bag of snacks to eat, just eat the snacks and do not have to relate to anyone else, but themselves. If a child has to attend to an adult to get each small piece of a snack, one at a time, the child is then attending and connecting several times to another person. Therefore, you hide the bag of snacks, and do not offer the bag to your child. Instead, you offer one small piece of food; one cheerio, one-half of a strawberry, one grape, one tiny piece of a cookie (not half, or the whole cookie), a tiny piece of a banana, one small piece of a favorite food, and hold it up to your nose. When you get a look in your direction, give that piece to your child. A moment later, ask "More?" or "Another One?" And at the same time offer another small piece, by holding it up to your nose, again. When your child looks again in your direction, quickly give the second piece. Try to get a look to your face (not eyes, just face) each time, and then quickly give another small piece. Repeat about five or seven times. Do that several times a day. Request a look or a facial expression, not a verbal response. Speaking will come later. If your child only focuses on the bag full of food, hide it while you offer the small bites. If your child does not look at you or the food, hold the food closer to the child's face in order to get attention, and then move it to your nose, as above. You can do the same with favorite toys, or anything your child wants at any time. The goal is improved attention to you; for your child to look at your face in order to get the desired object.

11. Give your child a brief playful tickle. Do what it takes to get your child's attention, even briefly. Blow bubbles, play with toys, roll a ball, hold a doll, make a funny face, play peek-a-boo, spin a ring or a small toy, sing a tune, or sing the first lines of a song. Repeat the play, the fun, and get your child's attention again. Maybe even get a smile or laugh at you. After a few seconds, repeat again, and get another "look," another bit of attention. Repeat again and again. Think of other ways to have fun, and to get your child's attention. Repeat them, on and off, all day long, as much as you can. The goal is improved attention to you; for your child to look at your face.

12. Using a screen motivator: A screen or electronic device can be used as an "attention getter" at first, and then soon used as a "motivator" to encourage engagement in back and forth attention with a person instead. Hold a small screen out so your child sees it. Then, move it up to your nose. When your child looks toward your face, even briefly, give a few seconds of time with the screen motivator. Then take it back and repeat, holding it to your nose again to see if your child wants it again. When your child looks toward your face again, even briefly, give it again for a few seconds. Take it back again. Hold it to your nose again, and repeat and repeat and repeat. You may even put your hand over the screen and block it until your child looks at you (to figure out what you are up to). Yes, your child may become upset. If he reaches for the screen and attempts to grab it out of your hand, block his hand and continue to hold it in front of your nose for a moment more. It may take several days for your child to understand, but once your child looks toward your face, immediately release your hand from the screen. Repeat holding it by your nose again in a minute, or two. Eventually redirect your child to a different interest, away from the screen, to and with you, as below. The goal is improved attention back to you, to your face, not only to the screen.

13. More ways to encourage "face-time." Get in front of your child. Your child should be encouraged to look in your direction each time something is wanted. You may say, "Look," but do not expect understanding of your words; demonstrate and attract instead. You can point to your nose, or your mouth to show your child where to look. You can gently turn his head so that your child looks at you. You can make a funny face or a silly noise.

Get a wanted toy, or a toy your child is playing with, and hold it to your nose, and offer it back to your child. If your child only looks at the toy, do not release it right away, and encourage your child to look at you first. When your child looks toward your face, even briefly, immediately give the toy. Repeat this over and over again. If your child just reaches for the object, and attempts to grab it out of your hand, block his hand and continue to hold the object in front of your nose for a while. Encourage a "look" towards your face. Then immediately give the toy. It may take several days for your child to understand. Hold several stacking cups together in your hand next to your face and offer them to your child. When your child looks at you, even briefly, give just one of the cups, and then offer another one in the same way. Get a look back to you before giving the cup. When your child looks at you before grabbing, give the next cup. Repeat with the third, fourth, and each next cup. Occasional "face-time" may happen in the first few weeks that you try, but it often takes several months until the "looks" become routine. It takes time for your child to figure out what is needed. Gradually over time, your child will look at your face to get your attention and then request something, instead of demanding the object before looking in your direction.

14. It takes time for your child to understand what you are doing and what you want him to do. Yes, it is natural that your child may get very upset until it is understood what is wanted. Allow for frustration and tantrums. When tantrums happen, don't fight. Step back. Stay calm. Allow the tantrum (if it is safe). After your child recovers, wait a minute, and then try again. Do not take, "No!" for a rejection; it is just a passing feeling at this time. Take it as a good response back to you. Don't take it personally. After the moment passes, wait a few seconds and try again, or try a different motivator, or try another method below. Do what it takes to keep the interaction going with you. Gradually, with time, your child will understand, and will look at you longer and longer. Eventually, your child will look at you to communicate, before you expect it. That is the goal!

15. Recognition: The goal is for your child to look in the direction of another person's face (not eyes, just face) when he wants something, and also when he is offered something. Your child should be directed (or helped by gentle touch) to look in someone's direction when help is wanted. Just grabbing and pulling you is not attending to you, but it

is just "using you" to get something that your child wants. When your child actually looks at your face as the first step, it is the beginning of making a connection, and attending to you, as an important person in your child's life. For example: instead of allowing your child to pull you to the door you may say "Door?" or "Help?" but do not move until your child looks toward your face, even briefly; the longer the better. Encourage your child to look in your direction by gently turning his head or holding your hand up near your face, or you look at your child's face, etc. Respond quickly, but briefly; take a step immediately after your child does look at you. Then repeat, and ask for a look again before each step. If your child puts something into your hand, without looking at you, keep your hand open; do not grab the object, let it fall. Encourage a look at you, and accept the object immediately after a look. The goal is for your child to recognize that when he does attend to you, as a person who can help, then help is given. As you get many more brief "looks" to you, the "looks" will become longer and more prolonged. The goal is sustained "looks" of attention, and recognition to you, instead of just focusing on a toy, flash cards, or a screen.

16. We all learn through play. In fact we learn best if the subject is interesting and fun. Try to play with your child on his interest level; do not always ask your child to do what interests you, the adult. Get down on the floor with your child and observe for a while. Watch and see what interests your child. Then, join in the play with your child. If your child enjoys watching wheels spin, you, too, may spin wheels for a while. Then you may try to spin it a bit slower or faster to get your child's attention to you. If your child likes to watch blocks fall off a table, move another block slowly to the edge so it falls. Your child may like that, and smile. You then ask "Again?" and repeat the action. Move another block even slower to the edge and wait a moment for a "look" to you before pushing it over. Repeat if it works. Try other things that interest your child. Try to make it fun. As you are accepted by your child in play, use the other methods described here to get more "looks," and to prolong the "look," the attention to your face. More important "redirection" ideas will come later.

17. Sing only the first line of a favorite song, pause and encourage a look in your direction before you continue. Sing songs together. Make up silly songs. Play music. Only play the first few lines of a favorite song, pause and require a look in your direction before you continue. Then, play the next line, pause and get another look. Repeat. Do not force the "look;" if it is difficult to get, go on with the song, but try again and again. It may take several attempts over several days.

18. Young children use their eyes more than their ears. They remember much better what they can't do when they are stopped, or where they are not allowed to go when they see physical boundaries, rather than where they are told not to go, or told not to do. The act of being stopped and redirected is very important. At this stage, you may be saying "Don't touch!" or "No!" several times a day, over several days or weeks. That means that talking to your child is not working now. Instead of just repeating words, cover, block, hide, or remove the attractive objects for now.

19. If your child likes to spin about, run in circles, hit his head, hit you, bite, pinch, or engage in nonfunctional repeated actions, it is recommended that you quickly interfere by gently placing your hand (or something) in the way and preventing him from continuing. And then immediately redirect his attention to you by being silly, or offering something else (even food), and encouraging another "look" or some response back to you. It is very important to immediately redirect his attention to you, as above. After several weeks of you interfering as above, you should see much less of the nonfunctional activity, and hopefully more attention to you.

Level 2: The Goal is For Your Child to Recognize That You Are Extremely Important!

Therefore, To Want to Get Your Attention!

1. Before learning to talk, your child needs to learn that you are extremely important, and that in order to talk to you, your child first needs to get your attention; your facial attention. Your child needs to look at your face to communicate, not just push you, pull you, hand things to you, or point.

2. Gatekeeping: It is important that your child must go to you or to the caretaker - interact with you or with the caretaker - in order to get what she wants. That way your child must recognize you, and attend to you to get something, not just get it by herself. As much as possible, remove the many toys and games that are sitting there for your child to attend to, instead of attending to you. Encourage your child to interact with you in order to get a toy, or anything, even food. The goal, now, is not for your child to reach out and to grab things, but for her to look towards you and to recognize that when she does attend to you as a person who has the thing she wants, then the object is given. This should be tried many times during the day, and at meal times. As you get many more brief "looks" to you, the "looks" will become longer. Soon the looks of attention will be long enough for your child to listen to what you say. The long term goal is sustained looks of attention to you. After that, back and forth non-verbal communication occurs.

3. Remember that most young children, especially those with joint attention delays, regulate their actions much more by what they see, rather than by what they hear. They use their eyes to watch what is going on, much more than listen to instructions. Children remember much better what they can't do, or where they are not allowed to go when they are stopped when they see physical boundaries, rather than where they are told not to go, or told not to do.

The act of being stopped and redirected is very important. A line on the floor, a change in flooring, a cover held in place, a blockade, moving an item out of view or hiding it, are some examples of boundaries. If you are saying, "No!" repeatedly, over several weeks, it is obvious that your child does not remember your stated limits. However, if you act and prevent, or you stop your child from doing something, or you place a boundary that stops your child, things will change.

4. If your child bites, hits or throws, try to anticipate the action and get there as fast as you can, and stop the action by moving her mouth, holding her hand or arm, and blocking and stopping the action before it continues. You may take the object away. Quickly redirect attention to you; sing a song, offer food, play a game or do something with your child. Yes there will be crying and tantrums at first. After several tries, your child will realize that there is a limit, and instead try to do something else. If your child attempts to climb on a table, immediately stop him and remove him, or block him, or move and keep the chair away. Then quickly redirect attention to you or a game or a toy or a sing a song with you. During these frustrating times, try to get your child's attention by just standing by and being present, or by redirecting to a different activity, offering help to do something else, or by consoling; not by punishing, and not by lecturing. Gradually, you then become more important.

5. Allowing your child to put hands on, and play with someone's face is not encouraged. Neither is playing with someone's eye glasses, or any other needed device. A child who plays with someone else's face, or own face, does not understand what a face is for. Many of these children also do not look very long at a face when trying to communicate. Gently stop the action, and try to redirect the action to you by using steps above or in level 1.

6. Try to make it fun for your child, and for you. We learn best when it is fun. Many of the methods in Level 1 also work to show your importance. Repeat some of the Level 1 methods that work well, and try to make them fun for your child.

7. Encourage less physical play (running about) and more recognition and attentive interaction to you, by asking you child to respond to questions. Many children enjoy physical play, so interact physically briefly at first, but then redirect the play locally: Let's bounce the ball. Let's march, like this. Let's tap on the table. Let's get some milk. Let's build a tower. Do you want this block? Offer the block. Tap her shoes and ask, "Where are your shoes?" Maybe say, "Let's play in this box." "Do you want the doll?" Offer the doll. Talk to your child's face. Get a look back to you with the answer. The answer is usually non-verbal, but may be verbal at times. The goal here is to get interaction between you both so that you become at least as important as a toy, or the physical play.

8. Try to see each play, instruction or activity as a series of multiple small parts. Pause between each part. Move only one step at a time when pulled or pushed. Request a look at your face. Then take another step and request another look. When that look happens, quickly take another step. Request another look, then take another step. Repeat and repeat. When your child comes over and puts something into your hand without looking at your face, do not hold the object, but keep your palm open, and let the object drop to the floor. When your child puts it into your hand again, repeat and let it fall. Move your empty hand to your face. When your child looks up at you, even briefly, then, accept the object. Open a container only partly, not fully. Pause for a look and facial expression. Then open a bit more. Get another look and facial expression. Play ball, pause, wait, get a look and facial expression, Resume play, and pause again.

9. If you child says, "No!" to you, do not take it as a rejection. Accept it as a strong feeling at that moment. It can be a very good response, as you are noticed as being important. Don't respond. Don't ask "Why?" Remember, don't take it personally. It will pass, and after it does, go on and continue the interaction. Be silly and make it fun, if you can. Continue to interact as before, and continue to get your child's attention.

10. The two biggest mistakes many parents make are 1) trying to reason with a child, and 2) becoming emotionally involved when a child does something wrong. That only encourages more wrong behavior. Try to step back and stay calm, as much as you can. Then, act and stop your child from getting into trouble. Block the way, or hold the door closed, stop the throwing, or move your child away from danger.

11. Play with your child and join in the same game as your child. If your child is playing with cars (or dolls, or blocks, etc.), you might say, "Oh that looks like fun." Then put your car gently in play. Or ask, "May I have a car, too?" Add another car if needed, or if accepted. Get a response back to you after each move. "May I have a different one?" Get another response back to you. If there is no response, you may take a car, and hold it up by your face, so your child has to look in your direction. When your child looks at you, immediately give the car back. Don't tease or force. If she pushes you or the car away, wait and try again and again. Allow your child to "win," and to have fun with you, so you become important.

12. Using small pictures may be helpful to show your child what comes next. Putting several small pictures (like flash cards) in order of a schedule low on a wall may be helpful to establish a routine. You may draw the pictures or find them: breakfast time, school time, toilet time, wash time, snack time, play time, dinner time, story time, bed time, etc. Show your child, and point to the next activity picture before doing it. This may help you become more important, and make it easier to direct your child to the next activity.

33

Level 3: The Goal is for Your Child to Want to Respond to You, and For You To Keep Your Child Engaged with You.

Speaking may occur, but is not yet the goal here.

1. With better attention over time, better speech will develop. The goal now is sustained "looks" of attention, recognition, responses, and following directions of an adult instead of focusing on a toy, flash cards, or a screen.

2. Following directions without attending to the speaker, does not assist in the development of appropriate speech, language and conversation development. In fact, it can hinder the development of back and forth communication. When you say, "Go get your shoes." does your child get the shoes without looking at your face or communicating back to you in any way? When you pick up the car keys and your child hears the noise, does he run to the door without looking at you or communicating back to you? In both cases the communication is only one way; from you to your child. There is no back and forth attention, back and forth communication.

3. Talk to your child in short, simple sentences. Try not to talk in paragraphs, but in one short phrase, or one brief instruction, at a time. Get attention; get a look, before giving an instruction or a direction. Examples: "Jimmy!" "Look." "Good."" Now, get your shoes." "Nina!" "Look." "Good." "We are going outside." "Carlos." "Look." "Good." "It is bath time." It is time to come in. It is time to get dressed, etc.   Make that a habit. Encourage many "looks," before doing anything, or asking anything. Eventually, your child will look at you first, to request your attention. That is the long term goal!

4. Prolong the attention: The goal is to keep your child engaged with you! Get your child's attention and wait a few seconds for him to look and connect with your face a bit longer than before. Once you have the attention directed to you, try to prolong it. Wait for a bit longer for the eye gaze, the "look," before giving an item. If the "look" is still brief, quickly, get your child's attention back again, and ask another related question. Over several months, build up the length of eye

gaze, recognition, attention, and "looks," back to you. Once your child looks in your direction, keep the attentive look refocused on you by building anticipation, pausing, asking more related questions, or engaging your child in a related interaction with you: "More milk?" "In this cup?" "This much?"; "More?" Each time, pause & prolong the attentive look as long as you can. Play peek-a-boo, or sing a song, but wait a few seconds after the first boo, or the first verse. Ask, "Do you want me to continue?" Encourage a look and a head nod or a facial expression or any gesture that shows a facial connection back to you. Then continue to the next verse. Stop again. Repeat the question. After another look of attention and/or a facial expression back to you, continue ... and repeat again. Once your child looks in your direction and attends to you a bit longer, try to keep that attentive look refocused on you by asking more questions, "Do you want more?" or "Here is the ball, do you want it?" or "Should I sing the next verse?" or "What should I do, now?" or "Are you sure? Gradually the "attentive looks" to you will become longer and longer, and your child will respond more and be able to follow more directions.

5. Prolong the interaction even more: You may also demonstrate (physically show) your child what to do so he understands. Put your toys away, like this. Now, let's jump, like this. Now, let's play ball. Oh, the doll needs shoes. Etc. Use action pictures, too. Also ask your child to point to objects that you name. Where is the dog? Where is the bear? Where is the horse? Where is your nose? Where is the banana? Fire truck?, airplane?, tree?, etc., etc. Use a picture book at times. First get your child's attention. Encourage your child to look at your face before you ask, or while you ask, and after the pointing. Repeat. You may ask, "Should I do more? "Two more?" "Do the truck again?" "Do you want to turn the page?" "Next page?" "Where is the snake?" "Go back to the dog?" "What is next?" Get attention to you again, and keep going. Your child may also verbally label the pictures, after there is some back and forth non-verbal connection.

6. Your child's speaking will come later. Even if your child says, "Yes!" or "Yeh!" that is not counted as attention, as your child may quickly discover that if he just says, "yes" or "yeh" without looking or attending, your child gets what he wants anyway. We are not trying to encourage speech, now, but trying to encourage prolonged attention and non-verbal responses. Therefore, at this time, it is the

attention, the "look," and the non-verbal facial expressions ("responses"), not the words, not the speech, that is wanted.

7. Interfere with the play, if it works. Briefly block the play. Put an obstacle in the way. Put your hand on a toy, or in the way. Put your hand on blocks so they can't be used in building. Put your hand over the hole on the toy so the shaped form won't go in. Gently block the road with a toy, or put your hand on a moving car to briefly stop it. Make your child deal with you (look at you, respond to you, gesture to you) to unblock the road, or to get the car moving again. Stop when your child becomes upset. If there are too many distractions nearby, your child may just move on to something else. If your child does not look back at you or insists in pulling your hand away without looking at you, go back to level 1, and build up more attention skills.

8. Play dumb, if it works. Act as if you do not understand when your child wants your help, or wants you to do something. Ask your child to show you. If your child puts something in your hand, ask, "What do I do with this?" Make a face, act surprised. Ask, "Does it go on the floor?" "On my head?" Or, "Show me where to put it." Before pouring milk, ask, "Do you want this?" "Does it go there?' "How much?" You can also make wrong moves; put the toy on your head, or on your foot, and see if your child corrects you. Play with a toy upside down or in some other way, and encourage your child to correct you. Point to your ear and ask "Is this my nose?" Get your child to work with you to figure out what to do. Non-verbal back and forth responses, back and forth non-verbal communication, is wanted, and if done, then some verbal responses are also acceptable.

9. Try to make it enjoyable for your child, and for you. Try to have fun. Play finger games, hand games –not running games –where your child must watch you and imitate what you do. Some examples: "Itsy Bitsy Spider;" "Where is Thumbkin? ... Here I am;" "Here is a church, and here is the steeple ...." or "Here is a bunny, with ears so funny, and here is the hole in the ground...." Maybe sing and act out Baby Shark. Then expand by asking questions that require a face to face response back to you, such as "More?" or "Where did she go?" The goal is to keep the back and forth non-verbal interaction going as long as you can.

10. Often playing music or a making up a song helps the child remember how to act. Songs and music are often used to encourage learning. The ABC song, Head Shoulders Knees and Toes, and the Clean-Up Song are some examples. Use music, rhymes, and songs as much as you can. Sometimes pause and wait for a few seconds after one or two lines, before continuing. That builds anticipation and connection. Ask, "Should I continue?" or "More?" Encourage a look and a nod, or a smile back to you in response. Then continue. Stretch out and expand the pauses, when possible, to create more anticipation and a longer look and connection to you.

11. Many children up to this level are not yet able to make choices. They are not yet able to choose one item from two. Many just "freeze" and get upset, or they want both. Don't force choices. Instead hold one item at a time up to your face, and ask if the child wants it, as in level one. Give it when your child looks in your direction and makes a facial gesture or head nod in response your question. Yes, you can demonstrate a smile, a facial gesture, a head nod or pointing. Don't accept reaching and grabbing. But be careful. Pointing away from you will cause your child to look away from your face. Yes, you should also encourage that look back to you with a facial expression. The look back to you with a facial expression is much more important than the pointing. Try more activities in levels one and two again to get that "look" back to you on a regular basis.

However, if your child does point and choses, and also does look back at you with a facial expression, offer choices at times. Always ask another question such as, "Is this what you want?" or "Really? or "This one?" Each time encourage another facial gesture or a head nod back to you in response. Give the item to your child when you get that facial gesture, smile, or a head nod back to you, not just when your child only points.

Level 4: The Goal is to Expand the Non-Verbal Joint Attention, and To Build Repeated Back and Forth Interactions; a Non-Verbal Conversation.

1. Non-verbal facial expressions; smiles, frowns, head nods, raise eyebrows, a wink of an eye lid, arm gestures, and pointing are extremely important in communication as they are the foundation of, and the building blocks toward, verbal communication. The goal here is to encourage your child to show multiple non-verbal connections back to you, in everyday situations.

2. Encourage multiple back and forth exchanges of communication (joint attention). Ask several questions. Ask your child to respond to the questions by non-verbal means. Example: Do you want to play this game? Do you want the red one? Where are the pieces? Where is the box? Do you want to wear this shirt? Where does this shoe go? On this foot ? Do I pour the milk into this cup? Just pour a little, then ask, "Do you want a little more?" Talk to your child's face. Get a look back to you and some non-verbal gesture with each answer; a smile, a head nod, a wave, a point, etc. You can demonstrate what you want your child to do by you doing the smiling, head nodding, etc., too.

3. Ask your child to make choices, if able, and respond back to you with facial expressions or gestures. It is the response back to you that is most important. Do not respond if your child just points, and does not look towards your face; go back to previous levels and work on responses. Do respond if your child responds back to your face with a facial expression, head nod or gesture, even if the pointing is not complete. Always ask several questions. "Do I pour the milk into this cup?" After your child responds you may ask again, "Or that cup?" You can ask, "Which shirt?" After a response, then ask again, "The red or the blue one?" Do you want long pants or the shorts? Big apple or little apple? This book or that one? This story or that one? Don't worry if your child does not make choices the way you would, or if she changes her mind. Always encourage a non-verbal gesture as above as an answer back to you, not just the pointing. Sometimes there may be a verbal response as well, but it is the non-verbal gestures that we are encouraging. Encourage non-verbal gestures.

4. Some of the methods in levels 2 & 3 can be used here again. Expand and prolong the back and forth non-verbal joint attention conversations as far as possible. Speech conversation is built upon the learned skills of non-verbal joint attention conversation, as described earlier.

5. Remember to try to make it fun (play) for your child, and for you. We all learn best when it is fun. Stop repeating an activity when she loses interest, and then begin encouraging again after a short while.

6. Redirect the play: Join in your child's play for a while. Then gently redirect so there is interaction between you both. Run with your child briefly, Stop, and then ask, "More?" or "Over here?" or say, "Now, you chase me." Make suggestions such as, "She looks tired, let's put the doll here. Ok?" or "May I put the dinosaur on this block?" You do it, and then ask your child to do something, too. After your child interacts with you for a while, and is showing some non-verbal joint attention, continue to try to increase the attention for a few more seconds, and also try to redirect the play a little bit. For example: Ask her to make the sound, or blow a bubble, instead of you doing it. Ask her to tickle you, instead of you doing the tickling. If your child focuses on spinning the wheels of a toy car, do that briefly with your child, then turn the car over and roll it back and forth on its wheels, and encourage your child to do that, too. Or you may ask or show your child to spin the wheels faster or slower with you. Now your child is interacting with you. Rolling a ball back and forth can be redirected by bouncing it once before rolling it back, and asking your child do that too, or by holding it in your hand for a few seconds longer, and asking your child to do that, too. Get a look each time, and a change in facial expressions, before each action, and each change in action. The "look" and a "change in facial expressions" is the important activity. Expand even more by asking more questions and keeping your child actively engaged with you – and looking at you as much as possible.

7. Read picture books to your child. Make up stories, if you can. Read a brief story at least three times a week, more, if you can. Repeating the same story several times is good, if wanted. Ask many questions, and get a facial response back to you each time. Also, alternating stories between new and previous read stories is good.

8. You point to a picture in a book, and ask a wrong question. Example, "Is this a rabbit?" (not). Get a facial response from your child. Then, ask another wrong question and get another facial response. Ask many questions. Expand by asking your child to point to any picture, and you can again label it either right or wrongly, "Is that a ...?" Be careful about asking your child to point to a distant object without also looking back to your face. Some children often prefer to look away rather than to look back to you.

9. At this level try not to ask, "What is that?" very often, because that question requires a verbal response. Try to ask questions that can be answered by non-verbal facial responses or body gestures: "Is that a bear?" Is that a car? Where is the elephant, airplane, etc.?" "Show me who is jumping?" "Is that silly?" "Again?" "Do you want more?" Etc.

10. Interfere with the play. See examples before. Put your finger in the way and briefly block an action of a toy or game. Quickly remove your finger when your child looks at you, and communicates with you. Expand even more. Stop when your child becomes upset.

11. When playing active physical games with your child such as ball play, running, climbing, etc., be sure to ask questions several times during the process, and encourage frequent facial responses and attention back to you. For example: Hold the ball for a few seconds and ask, "Do you want it back?" or "Do I toss it over there?" A little while later, ask, again, "Should we keep playing?" or "How about doing it this way?" Encourage a look back to you after each question. As soon as you get a look and an appropriate expression back to you, continue playing. Continue with many more questions and/or redirections so your child interacts back and forth with you several times.

12. Ask a 3 year or older old child to point to who is walking, who is talking, who is sitting, who is sleeping, who is eating; words that end with "ing." Then, once or twice, you ask her to point what she wants to point to, and you label the action. Each time you ask if you should do it again, and get a "look" and/or a facial gesture back in your direction. This encourages back and forth non-verbal conversation. We are not encouraging your child to speak, but if it does happen it is good as long as it is accompanied with more non-verbal back and forth responses. Speaking without non-verbal gestures back to you is not encouraged now.

13. Encourage creative and pretend play. Create a "game," with your child, such as, "Show me how rabbits hop." Your child tries to hop. "The dinosaur is hungry. Can you give him some food?" Your child pretends to feed the dinosaur. "Are you a tiger?" Your child makes an angry face or roars. "Are you a frog?" Your child pretends to be a frog. "Can you pretend to fly?" "Pretend that you are asleep?" Can the superhero walk, jump, fly? "How does the airplane fly?" The stuffed bear wants to play, eat, drink, read, or rest. The toy horse is thirsty, hungry, tired. The horse wants to say hello to the dog; your child places the animals face to face. The bear wants to go for a ride in/on the car, train, etc. Can you pretend to drive a car? Can you pretend to ....? The baby doll is cold, hungry, happy, sad, or wants to dance. The baby doll is tired; night-night. Etc. After the pretend action, ask again, "Did she eat the food?" or "Did she go to sleep?" Each time encourage a facial response back to you during or just after the action.

14. You can do art with your child. Use coloring books or make it free form. Use various colors. Don't let her be alone for long. It is important to take turns drawing, and to ask her many questions (such as, "My turn?" May I use the blue?" "Over here?" Etc.) to encourage facial responses or gestures back to you as above, so your child interacts back and forth with you several times. Use art, music, sing songs back and forth, and dance together. Encourage facial expressions, smile, be happy, and make funny faces back and forth at each other. Keep the back and forth responses going.

Level 5: The Goal is to Add Appropriate Speech on to the Non-Verbal [Joint Attention] Conversation.

1. At this level your child is able to focus on your face, recognize that you are important, wants to interact with you, and understands and uses non-verbal joint attention. Your child pays attention to you (much of the time, no one pays attention all of the time) and follows many directions. You should notice several facial responses, and back and forth non-verbal communication much more of the time, such as head nods, smiles, frowns, pointing, or gestures in response to each of your series of questions, or instructions.

2. At this level your child is able to respond his name most of the time, follow many "one step" directions without your hand signals, such as bring me your shoes, put the ball on the truck, give the book to mom/dad, open the box, put it on the table, etc. He can point to several body parts, and point to several objects: Where is the dog?, the bear?, the book?, the car?, and other familiar objects. At this level your child may like to imitate you, and stretch his arms up high when you play "so big!" He may make facial expressions, the same smiley faces that you do, and attempt to copy something you say by jabbering with a similar tone of voice, or maybe say more words.

3. At this level of development, your child is able to learn more, and will get the most benefit from one-on-one speech and language therapy. Many therapists understand how to find the level of your child's abilities, and at what level to begin therapy. They often begin by finding what basic foundation skills your child has already mastered and understands. Once those skills are known, they can be built upon, and the next steps will be learned more easily.

4. Encourage talking by beginning with your child's non-vocal skills. One example: His almost three year old daughter said only 3 words. The father was asked to gently playfully tickle her so she would look at him. She looked at him. Then, the father was asked to ask her if he should stop. He did. She looked at him and nodded her head for yes, but said no words. The father was then instructed to ask her to say, "Stop." The father then said, "Say stop." And she responded, "Stop!" And he immediately stopped. That was the first time his daughter said that word.

5. Don't bribe your child to say words. Do not tell your child," I will give you the banana if you say banana." If your child could say the word, he would. Instead, play games with your child such as playing with a ball. During the play, offer the ball, and say, "Say 'ball.'" Sometimes your child will say the word, other times not. Using creative and pretend play also helps. When you put a blanket over the doll, you say, "The doll is going to bed, say 'night-night.'" Or you move the horse and say, "The horse is saying Hi to the cow, say 'Hi' or 'Hi cow;'" Or you can feed the doll and say, "The baby wants more milk, say 'Milk' or 'More milk'" or … more water, say 'water,' Etc.

6. Talk to your child and explain what you are doing: "We are washing our hands." "We are putting on our jackets." "We are walking to the park." "See that bird? It is on the branch." "That is a big truck. … A white truck." Also ask many questions: "Where is the soap?" "Where is the towel?" "Is that a dump truck?" "Where are the doors?" "Where is the driver?" Get a non-verbal or a verbal response, and keep the back and forth conversation going as long as you can.

7. Continue to read picture books as much as possible. Make up stories, if you can. Read a brief story at least three times a week, more, if you can. Repeating the same story several times is good. Describe what is happening in the pictures. Ask many questions: What is the girl doing? What is going to happen next? Who is hiding? Did you like that? Encourage both a non-verbal and a verbal response back to you.

About the author:

John D. Michael, MD is a Staff Physician at the Golden Gate Regional Center, San Francisco, CA & Clinical Professor of Pediatrics (Ret) UCSF School of Medicine, University of California, San Francisco, CA

References:

1. Stanley I. Greenspan, M.D. and Stuart G. Shanker, D. Phil.,*The First Idea, How Symbols, Language, and Intelligence Evolved from our Primitive Ancestors to Modern Humans,* Da Capo Press, 2004

2. Stanley I. Greenspan & Serena Wieder, *Engaging Autism: Using the Floortime Approach to Help Children Relate, Communicate, and Think,* A Merloyd Lawrence Book, Da Capo Press, 2007

3. John Michael, MD, and Jasna Cowan, MS, CCC-SLP, *A Different Way to Assess Receptive Language.* Looking at a child's receptive language in a new way can shed light on eligibility and the road to therapy, ADVANCE for Speech-Language Pathologists and Audiologists, Vol. 20, Issue 5, March 8, 2010, P20.

4. John Michael, MD, and Jasna Cowan, MS, CCC-SSLP, *Receptive Language*, ADVANCE for Speech-Language Pathologists and Audiologists, Vol. 20, Issue 15, July 26, 2010, P21. Editor's note: Due to strong reader interest in their first article, "A Different Way to Assess Receptive Language" [ADVANCE, 20 (5): 20], the authors expand on the topic.

5. Jasna Cowan, MS, CCC-SLP, and John Michael, MD, *Receptive Language: Communication Therapy*, ADVANCE for Speech-Language Pathologists and Audiologists (on Website), July 27, 2011

6. Sally Rogers & Geraldine Dawson, *Early Start Denver Model for Young Children with Autism,* The Guilford Press, NY, 2010.

Appendix:

"How to teach your child to attend longer to you" 48, 52, 56
A brief selection from Attention Therapy.
Brief hand-outs for caretakers and preschool,
if appropriate.

How to teach your child to ATTEND LONGER TO YOU and to develop back and forth communication with you
Copyright John D. Michael, MD, 12/2020

This is a brief selection from Attention Therapy

Learning to pay attention: a child must first develop the ability to understand the importance of looking at and listening to the speaker. This takes time to learn. Then, a child must engage in appropriate back and forth non-verbal attention and responses; face expressions, smiles, head nods, etc. back to you. This will also take time to learn. Only after that will good verbal conversation develop fully.

The goal is sustained attention & response, back to you!

1) Look for recognition, visual attention, looking toward your face (not eye contact), facial expressions, gestures, and other non-verbal responses that show attention to you and with you (not to or with a toy).

2) **Talk to your child's face**. Get in front of your child. Get attention before giving directions! Be a model for your child. Talk clearly and slowly. Make a noise. Clap your hands. Gently touch your child. Turn his head to you. Call her name. Point to your nose, mouth, or face. Smile. Nod your head. Make a funny face. Hold/move a favorite object to your nose or on your head and ask, "Do you want this?" Give it when a "look" of attention occurs, not when he only reaches out and grabs it. If he only reaches out to grab it, block his hand and encourage a look to you. Get his attention, get a look back to you, even briefly & try to prolong it. Hold more objects to your nose, and quickly give each when your child looks at you. Eventually get more facial responses, back to you. Repeat and repeat.

3) With food: Offer only one small bite of food (the size of one Cheerio or one blueberry) at first, not the whole thing; "Do you want more?" Get a non-verbal look at you. Give one small bite or one more blueberry. Again ask, "More?" Get another non-verbal look back to you. Then, give just a bit more. Ask again. Get another look, but a bit longer. Keep this going at each meal and snack in order to get looks and non-verbal responses. Repeat and repeat. After your child is looking and attending, offer a cup with very little liquid and ask if you should put something

more into it. Get a non-verbal facial response (a smile, a gesture, head nod) back to you. Then respond quickly and add just a bit more liquid. Then ask again. Do the same with food. Continue asking and getting responses again and again.

4) With toys: Hold a ball in your hand next to your nose, and offer it to your child. If your child looks at the ball, hold it tight. If the look is at you, even briefly, give the ball. You can point to your nose, or your mouth to show your child where to look. You can gently turn her head up so that she looks at you. You can make a funny face or a silly noise. Offer a part of a toy, or just one car, and then ask, "Do you want another one?" Get another toy and offer it by your nose to your child. If your child only looks at the toy, do not release it right away and encourage your child to look at you first. Repeat this over and over again. Another example: Hold several stacking cups together in your hand next to your face and offer them to your child. When your child looks at you, even briefly, give just one of the cups. Then offer another one in the same way. Get a look back to you before giving each cup. When your child looks at you, before grabbing, give the next cup. Repeat with the third, fourth, and each next cup.

5) Occasionally "face-time" may happen in the first few weeks that you try, but it often takes several months until the "looks" become routine. It takes time for your child to figure out what is needed. Gradually over time, your child will look at your face to get your attention and then request something, instead of demanding the object before looking in your direction.

6) Sing songs, play music, and use gestures. Use feelings and facial expressions such as a happy voice, cry, laugh, smile, etc. Sing just one line then ask, "More?" Encourage a response, a smile, a nod, back to you. Then play one more line. Smile at your child's face in order to get him to smile back at you. Repeat. Play peek-a-boo in order to get different facial expressions. Of course your child will laugh when having fun, but that is not enough. Encourage your child to show connection to you, to look at your face, to use non-verbal expressions and body language in everyday situations. Ask many questions, "Having fun?" "Want more?" and each time get a look and a facial expression back to you.

7) Play with your child. Join in with your child's play for a while. Encourage less physical play (running about, ball play, etc.) and encourage more recognition-play by following your basic directions over and over, responding to your many questions, "Should I run/jump again? Now, let's do it this way." "Do you want that again? - Where?" Each time, encourage a look at your face; a look back to you, plus a non-verbal response (gesture, smile, head nod, pointing, etc.).

8) After getting many consistent non-verbal responses, try asking, "Do I put it on the table or in the cup?" "No, then where should I put it?" (shakes head or points) "Here or there?" Make it silly if necessary; "On your nose or on the plate?" Your child should be encouraged to look at your face each time something is asked for or is wanted. Ignore verbal responses (Yeh, Uh, Ma, etc.), but do respond quickly to looks & non-verbal facial responses.

9) After your child frequently responds to you, Play dumb. Act as if you do not understand and ask your child to show you. Then smile, agree, compliment your child and cooperate with the request if you can. Ask dumb questions: "I do not understand. Show me." "What do I do with this? Show me." "Where does it go, now?" "Do you want it in a cup or on a plate?" Get a non-verbal response to your questions! If there are 2 items "Which one? Show me." "Where do I put it? On your head?" "Why not" "What do I do next?" "Do you want help?" Get non-verbal looks or responses back to you. Make the wrong move, "Do I put it here (in the wrong place)?" "Get another non-verbal response. Then, "Show me where to put it." (non-verbal response) "Does it really go there?" (response) How about here?" (response) Continue… Each time encourage a look at your face; a look back to you, and a non-verbal gesture back to you – without talking!

10) Interfere with the play. Put obstacles into the play, gently. Block the road with a toy bus, etc. Hold a toy, keep it from moving. Make your child deal with you by encouraging a look at your face; a look back to you, and a facial gesture. Then you remove the obstacle. "Should I give it back to you?" "Do you want this?" "Where does it go? Show me." Each time encourage a look at your face; a look back to you, plus a non-verbal gesture back to you in response.

11) Discourage your child from non-functional activities: hurting or hitting himself & others, throwing toys, lining up toys in a row instead of playing with them, spinning about, waking/running in circles, spinning wheels or toys, focusing on things that turn or spin. Gently touch your child, interfere and stop the action, then immediately redirect to some other interest with you, as mentioned above.

12) Allow for frustration and non-cooperation, and tantrums. Give in, rest, then repeat the requests. Do not treat "No!" as a rejection, but just as a passing feeling at the time. It is a good response! After a few minutes, repeat the above requests.

At first, do not frequently ask, "What is that?" because this question requires a verbal response, but do accept a non-verbal response (facial gestures, head nod, pointing, etc.) if given. Do what it takes to keep the interaction going with you! = Back and forth between you two!

Expand and prolong the interactions above to you, and with you! Remember that the goal is sustained looks of attention to you (not to a toy), to regularly respond back to you, and then to engage in multiple steps of back and forth non-verbal responses with you. This is basic. After that is mastered, your child will learn to talk to you, and talk with you.

Hey there, Pay Attention.

Pay Attention to Attention Therapy!

How to teach your child to ATTEND LONGER TO YOU and to develop back and forth communication with you

This is a brief selection from Attention Therapy

Learning to pay attention: a child must first develop the ability to understand the importance of looking at and listening to the speaker. This takes time to learn. Then, a child must engage in appropriate back and forth non-verbal attention and responses; face expressions, smiles, head nods, etc. back to you. This will also take time to learn. Only after that will good verbal conversation develop fully.

The goal is sustained attention & response, back to you!

1) Look for recognition, visual attention, looking toward your face (not eye contact), facial expressions, gestures, and other non-verbal responses that show attention to you and with you (not to or with a toy).

2) **Talk to your child's face**. Get in front of your child. Get attention before giving directions! Be a model for your child. Talk clearly and slowly. Make a noise. Clap your hands. Gently touch your child. Turn his head to you. Call her name. Point to your nose, mouth, or face. Smile. Nod your head. Make a funny face. Hold/move a favorite object to your nose or on your head and ask, "Do you want this?" Give it when a "look" of attention occurs, not when he only reaches out and grabs it. If he only reaches out to grab it, block his hand and encourage a look to you. Get his attention, get a look back to you, even briefly & try to prolong it. Hold more objects to your nose, and quickly give each when your child looks at you. Eventually get more facial responses, back to you. Repeat and repeat.

3) With food: Offer only one small bite of food (the size of one Cheerio or one blueberry) at first, not the whole thing; "Do you want more?" Get a non-verbal look at you. Give one small bite or one more blueberry. Again ask, "More?" Get another non-verbal look back to you. Then, give just a bit more. Ask again. Get another look, but a bit longer. Keep this going at each meal and snack in order to get looks and non-verbal responses. Repeat and repeat. After your child is looking and attending, offer a cup with very little liquid and ask if you should put something

more into it. Get a non-verbal facial response (a smile, a gesture, head nod) back to you. Then respond quickly and add just a bit more liquid. Then ask again. Do the same with food. Continue asking and getting responses again and again.

4) With toys: Hold a ball in your hand next to your nose, and offer it to your child. If your child looks at the ball, hold it tight. If the look is at you, even briefly, give the ball. You can point to your nose, or your mouth to show your child where to look. You can gently turn her head up so that she looks at you. You can make a funny face or a silly noise. Offer a part of a toy, or just one car, and then ask, "Do you want another one?" Get another toy and offer it by your nose to your child. If your child only looks at the toy, do not release it right away and encourage your child to look at you first. Repeat this over and over again. Another example: Hold several stacking cups together in your hand next to your face and offer them to your child. When your child looks at you, even briefly, give just one of the cups. Then offer another one in the same way. Get a look back to you before giving each cup. When your child looks at you, before grabbing, give the next cup. Repeat with the third, fourth, and each next cup.

5) Occasionally "face-time" may happen in the first few weeks that you try, but it often takes several months until the "looks" become routine. It takes time for your child to figure out what is needed. Gradually over time, your child will look at your face to get your attention and then request something, instead of demanding the object before looking in your direction.

6) Sing songs, play music, and use gestures. Use feelings and facial expressions such as a happy voice, cry, laugh, smile, etc. Sing just one line then ask, "More?" Encourage a response, a smile, a nod, back to you. Then play one more line. Smile at your child's face in order to get him to smile back at you. Repeat. Play peek-a-boo in order to get different facial expressions. Of course your child will laugh when having fun, but that is not enough. Encourage your child to show connection to you, to look at your face, to use non-verbal expressions and body language in everyday situations. Ask many questions, "Having fun?" "Want more?" and each time get a look and a facial expression back to you.

7) Play with your child. Join in with your child's play for a while. Encourage less physical play (running about, ball play, etc.) and encourage more recognition-play by following your basic directions over and over, responding to your many questions, "Should I run/jump again? Now, let's do it this way." "Do you want that again? - Where?" Each time, encourage a look at your face; a look back to you, plus a non-verbal response (gesture, smile, head nod, pointing, etc.).

8) After getting many consistent non-verbal responses, try asking, "Do I put it on the table or in the cup?" "No, then where should I put it?" (shakes head or points) "Here or there?" Make it silly if necessary; "On your nose or on the plate?" Your child should be encouraged to look at your face each time something is asked for or is wanted. Ignore verbal responses (Yeh, Uh, Ma, etc.), but do respond quickly to looks & non-verbal facial responses.

9) After your child frequently responds to you, Play dumb. Act as if you do not understand and ask your child to show you. Then smile, agree, compliment your child and cooperate with the request if you can. Ask dumb questions: "I do not understand. Show me." "What do I do with this? Show me." "Where does it go, now?" "Do you want it in a cup or on a plate?" Get a non-verbal response to your questions! If there are 2 items "Which one? Show me." "Where do I put it? On your head?" "Why not" "What do I do next?" "Do you want help?" Get non-verbal looks or responses back to you. Make the wrong move, "Do I put it here (in the wrong place)?" "Get another non-verbal response. Then, "Show me where to put it." (non-verbal response) "Does it really go there?" (response) How about here?" (response) Continue… Each time encourage a look at your face; a look back to you, and a non-verbal gesture back to you – without talking!

10) Interfere with the play. Put obstacles into the play, gently. Block the road with a toy bus, etc. Hold a toy, keep it from moving. Make your child deal with you by encouraging a look at your face; a look back to you, and a facial gesture. Then you remove the obstacle. "Should I give it back to you?" "Do you want this?" "Where does it go? Show me." Each time encourage a look at your face; a look back to you, plus a non-verbal gesture back to you in response.

11) Discourage your child from non-functional activities: hurting or hitting himself & others, throwing toys, lining up toys in a row instead of playing with them, spinning about, waking/running in circles, spinning wheels or toys, focusing on things that turn or spin. Gently touch your child, interfere and stop the action, then immediately redirect to some other interest with you, as mentioned above.

12) Allow for frustration and non-cooperation, and tantrums. Give in, rest, then repeat the requests. Do not treat "No!" as a rejection, but just as a passing feeling at the time. It is a good response! After a few minutes, repeat the above requests.

At first, do not frequently ask, "What is that?" because this question requires a verbal response, but do accept a non-verbal response (facial gestures, head nod, pointing, etc.) if given. Do what it takes to keep the interaction going with you! = Back and forth between you two!

Expand and prolong the interactions above to you, and with you! Remember that the goal is sustained looks of attention to you (not to a toy), to regularly respond back to you, and then to engage in multiple steps of back and forth non-verbal responses with you. This is basic. After that is mastered, your child will learn to talk to you, and talk with you.

Hey there, Pay Attention.

Pay Attention to Attention Therapy!

55

How to teach your child to ATTEND LONGER TO YOU and to develop back and forth communication with you

Copyright John D. Michael, MD, 12/2020

This is a brief selection from Attention Therapy

Learning to pay attention: a child must first develop the ability to understand the importance of looking at and listening to the speaker. This takes time to learn. Then, a child must engage in appropriate back and forth non-verbal attention and responses; face expressions, smiles, head nods, etc. back to you. This will also take time to learn. Only after that will good verbal conversation develop fully.

The goal is sustained attention & response, back to you!

1) Look for recognition, visual attention, looking toward your face (not eye contact), facial expressions, gestures, and other non-verbal responses that show attention to you and with you (not to or with a toy).

2) **Talk to your child's face**. Get in front of your child. Get attention before giving directions! Be a model for your child. Talk clearly and slowly. Make a noise. Clap your hands. Gently touch your child. Turn his head to you. Call her name. Point to your nose, mouth, or face. Smile. Nod your head. Make a funny face. Hold/move a favorite object to your nose or on your head and ask, "Do you want this?" Give it when a "look" of attention occurs, not when he only reaches out and grabs it. If he only reaches out to grab it, block his hand and encourage a look to you. Get his attention, get a look back to you, even briefly & try to prolong it. Hold more objects to your nose, and quickly give each when your child looks at you. Eventually get more facial responses, back to you. Repeat and repeat.

3) With food: Offer only one small bite of food (the size of one Cheerio or one blueberry) at first, not the whole thing; "Do you want more?" Get a non-verbal look at you. Give one small bite or one more blueberry. Again ask, "More?" Get another non-verbal look back to you. Then, give just a bit more. Ask again. Get another look, but a bit longer. Keep this going at each meal and snack in order to get looks and non-verbal responses. Repeat and repeat. After your child is looking and attending, offer a cup with very little liquid and ask if you should put something

more into it. Get a non-verbal facial response (a smile, a gesture, head nod) back to you. Then respond quickly and add just a bit more liquid. Then ask again. Do the same with food. Continue asking and getting responses again and again.

4) With toys: Hold a ball in your hand next to your nose, and offer it to your child. If your child looks at the ball, hold it tight. If the look is at you, even briefly, give the ball. You can point to your nose, or your mouth to show your child where to look. You can gently turn her head up so that she looks at you. You can make a funny face or a silly noise. Offer a part of a toy, or just one car, and then ask, "Do you want another one?" Get another toy and offer it by your nose to your child. If your child only looks at the toy, do not release it right away and encourage your child to look at you first. Repeat this over and over again. Another example: Hold several stacking cups together in your hand next to your face and offer them to your child. When your child looks at you, even briefly, give just one of the cups. Then offer another one in the same way. Get a look back to you before giving each cup. When your child looks at you, before grabbing, give the next cup. Repeat with the third, fourth, and each next cup.

5) Occasionally "face-time" may happen in the first few weeks that you try, but it often takes several months until the "looks" become routine. It takes time for your child to figure out what is needed. Gradually over time, your child will look at your face to get your attention and then request something, instead of demanding the object before looking in your direction.

6) Sing songs, play music, and use gestures. Use feelings and facial expressions such as a happy voice, cry, laugh, smile, etc. Sing just one line then ask, "More?" Encourage a response, a smile, a nod, back to you. Then play one more line. Smile at your child's face in order to get him to smile back at you. Repeat. Play peek-a-boo in order to get different facial expressions. Of course your child will laugh when having fun, but that is not enough. Encourage your child to show connection to you, to look at your face, to use non-verbal expressions and body language in everyday situations. Ask many questions, "Having fun?" "Want more?" and each time get a look and a facial expression back to you.

7) Play with your child. Join in with your child's play for a while. Encourage less physical play (running about, ball play, etc.) and encourage more recognition-play by following your basic directions over and over, responding to your many questions, "Should I run/jump again? Now, let's do it this way." "Do you want that again? - Where?" Each time, encourage a look at your face; a look back to you, plus a non-verbal response (gesture, smile, head nod, pointing, etc.).

8) After getting many consistent non-verbal responses, try asking, "Do I put it on the table or in the cup?" "No, then where should I put it?" (shakes head or points) "Here or there?" Make it silly if necessary; "On your nose or on the plate?" Your child should be encouraged to look at your face each time something is asked for or is wanted. Ignore verbal responses (Yeh, Uh, Ma, etc.), but do respond quickly to looks & non-verbal facial responses.

9) After your child frequently responds to you, Play dumb. Act as if you do not understand and ask your child to show you. Then smile, agree, compliment your child and cooperate with the request if you can. Ask dumb questions: "I do not understand. Show me." "What do I do with this? Show me." "Where does it go, now?" "Do you want it in a cup or on a plate?" Get a non-verbal response to your questions! If there are 2 items "Which one? Show me." "Where do I put it? On your head?" "Why not" "What do I do next?" "Do you want help?" Get non-verbal looks or responses back to you. Make the wrong move, "Do I put it here (in the wrong place)?" "Get another non-verbal response. Then, "Show me where to put it." (non-verbal response) "Does it really go there?" (response) How about here?" (response) Continue... Each time encourage a look at your face; a look back to you, and a non-verbal gesture back to you – without talking!

10) Interfere with the play. Put obstacles into the play, gently. Block the road with a toy bus, etc. Hold a toy, keep it from moving. Make your child deal with you by encouraging a look at your face; a look back to you, and a facial gesture. Then you remove the obstacle. "Should I give it back to you?" "Do you want this?" "Where does it go? Show me." Each time encourage a look at your face; a look back to you, plus a non-verbal gesture back to you in response.

11) Discourage your child from non-functional activities: hurting or hitting himself & others, throwing toys, lining up toys in a row instead of playing with them, spinning about, waking/running in circles, spinning wheels or toys, focusing on things that turn or spin. Gently touch your child, interfere and stop the action, then immediately redirect to some other interest with you, as mentioned above.

12) Allow for frustration and non-cooperation, and tantrums. Give in, rest, then repeat the requests. Do not treat "No!" as a rejection, but just as a passing feeling at the time. It is a good response! After a few minutes, repeat the above requests.

At first, do not frequently ask, "What is that?" because this question requires a verbal response, but do accept a non-verbal response (facial gestures, head nod, pointing, etc.) if given. Do what it takes to keep the interaction going with you! = Back and forth between you two!

Expand and prolong the interactions above to you, and with you! Remember that the goal is sustained looks of attention to you (not to a toy), to regularly respond back to you, and then to engage in multiple steps of back and forth non-verbal responses with you. This is basic. After that is mastered, your child will learn to talk to you, and talk with you.

Hey there, Pay Attention.

Pay Attention to Attention Therapy!

Made in United States
North Haven, CT
29 May 2024

53094734R00037